Stamping
F · U · N
PETRA BOASE

ACROPOLIS
BOOKS

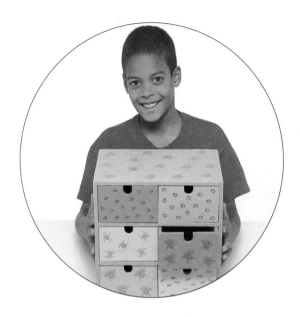

For Biba

The author would like to thank Lisa Edwardes for her help in the studio.

First published in 1996 by Lorenz Books

Lorenz Books is an imprint of Anness Publishing Limited, 1 Boundary Row, London SE1 8HP

© 1996 Anness Publishing Limited
Distributed in Canada by Raincoast Books Limited

ISBN 1 85967 225 6

A CIP catalogue record for this book is available from the British Library.

Publisher: Joanna Lorenz
Senior Editor, Children's Books: Caroline Beattie
Photographer: John Freeman
Designers: Tony Sambrook and Edward Kinsey

Printed and bound by Star Standard, Singapore.

Introduction

Stamping is a very creative form of decoration and is great fun to do. If you are unable to buy any ready-made rubber stamps, don't panic because on pages 9–11 we show you how to make your very own range, using all sorts of different materials, which you will probably find lying around your home.

The projects in this book are very exciting and I'm sure after reading only a few of them you will be eager to get to work. However, before you do, it is very important to organize yourself: make sure that you have covered the surface you are working on with an old cloth or with pieces of newspaper, and that all the equipment you need is close at hand.

When you are using ready-made rubber stamps or your home-made ones, remember to wash them gently after use, and in between each print when you are using a different coloured ink. Dry them gently with a towel. Also never forget to put the lids on the printing inks, otherwise they might dry up. However, the important thing about stamping is to let your imagination run wild and to have lots and lots of fun!

Petra Boase

3

Contents

Materials &
Equipment

Fabric ink pens

Fabric ink

Pigment ink pads

STAMPS WITH HANDLES

These are great if you want to get a firm hold of the stamp when you are using it to print.

WOODEN BLOCK STAMPS

These are the heaviest stamps and they feel very stable when you print with them.

ROLLER STAMPS

These are long rubber stamps that are on a roller. You roll them first on the ink pad and then roll it over the surface on which you want to print. The print will be in a line. The longer you want the print to be, the more ink you have to apply to the stamp.

RUBBER STAMPS (PART OF A KIT)

This is probably the cheapest way to buy rubber stamps. The kits usually have a theme, for instance sea life, and within the kit you get lots of different stamps.

FABRIC INK STAMP PAD

This is a fabric pad and you pour the fabric ink onto it. When the ink runs out you simply add more ink. You will need a separate pad for each different coloured ink.

FABRIC INK

This comes in a bottle and you pour it onto a fabric ink pad. Always make sure the lid is screwed on tightly so that if it falls over it won't leak and make a mess.

FABRIC INK PENS

These look like felt pens. You simply colour in areas of the stamp using a mixture of colours and then print onto fabric. Remember to put the lids on after use, otherwise they will dry up.

PRINTING FELT PENS

These also look like felt pens. You simply colour in the rubber stamp, using as many colours as you want to, and then print onto paper or card. Remember to put the lids on after use.

INK PADS

These come in an assortment of colours and are used to colour stamp to print on paper and card.

PIGMENT INK PADS

These use a different sort of ink and the colours are very strong and brigh Use on card, paper and wood.

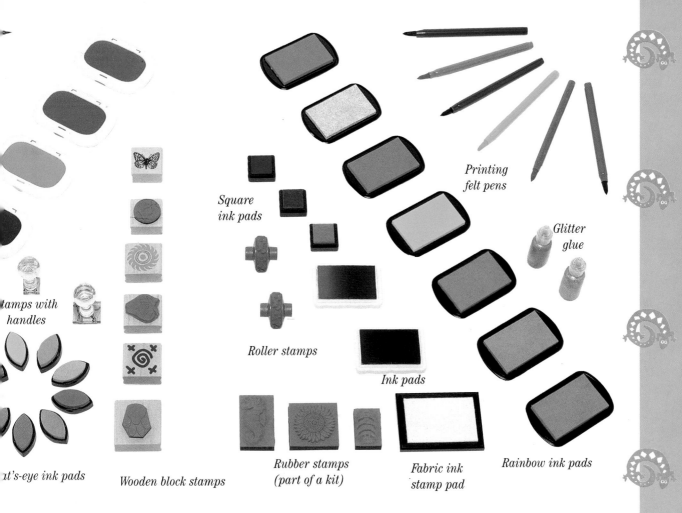

Square ink pads

Printing felt pens

Glitter glue

amps with handles

Roller stamps

Ink pads

it's-eye ink pads

Wooden block stamps

Rubber stamps (part of a kit)

Fabric ink stamp pad

Rainbow ink pads

AINBOW INK PADS

hese are ink pads with several inks
them. When you print the stamp,
e print will be multi-coloured.

AT'S-EYE INK PADS

se an assortment of colours and dab
em onto the rubber stamp to create
multi-coloured print.

SQUARE INK PADS

These are very good if you only have
very small rubber stamps. They are
also useful if you want to dab different
colours onto the stamp to create a
multi-coloured print.

GLITTER GLUE

This is great for decorating your
stamped prints, but allow it to dry
thoroughly before touching it or else
it will smudge.

Creative Ideas

Rubber stamps come in all shapes and sizes and in an enormous range of images and patterns. These are a few examples of different effects you can get from different colours and patterns. A pigment ink stamp pad was used for all the prints here.

1 Use a roller stamp to decorate a ribbon for a present or even to put in your hair.

2 You can use an ordinary stamp to give the same effect as a roller, by printing the motif several times in a row.

3 Repeat a motif several times in rows to give a neat pattern.

4 Repeat a motif in a more scattered way to give a freer pattern.

6 Use colours that are quite close to each other to give a subtle print.

7 Use contrasting inks and papers to give a very bright effect.

5 Experiment with different-coloured inks and papers. Pink ink on blue paper could give you a purple print, whereas blue ink on pink paper could still give you a blue print.

Home-Made Stamps

Making your own stamps means that you get your very own unique motifs.

SAFETY FIRST!
To make some home-made stamps, the shape needs to be cut out with a craft knife – ALWAYS ask an adult to do this for you.

STRING

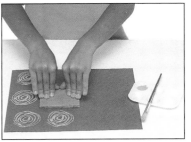

1 Cut out a square of thick card. Paint glue over the card and, starting in the middle of it, begin to coil a length of string into a spiral shape. Cut the end of the string when you have made your shape.

2 Paint the string with paint (or with fabric paint) and print, pressing down firmly. You will need to re-apply the paint onto the string for each print. String gives you designs with nice fine lines.

CORD

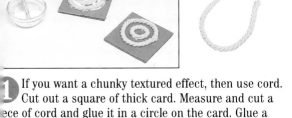

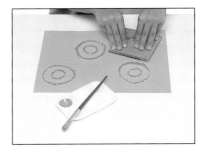

1 If you want a chunky textured effect, then use cord. Cut out a square of thick card. Measure and cut a piece of cord and glue it in a circle on the card. Glue a shorter length of cord in a circle in the middle of the other circle. Leave the glue to harden.

2 Paint the cord with paint or, if you are printing onto fabric, with fabric paint, and print, pressing down firmly. You will need to re-apply paint onto the cord for each print. Don't put too much paint on the cord, so that the design is nice and clear.

CARDBOARD

1 Cut a piece of thick card into a square. Cut another piece of card into whatever shape you want and glue it onto the card square. Allow the glue to harden.

2 Stamp the card shape onto a pigment ink pad and print, pressing down firmly. If you are printing on fabric, remember to use a fabric ink pad. Re-apply the ink after each print.

RUBBER

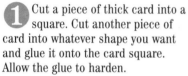

1 Draw a shape on one side of the rubber with a biro or a pencil. Ask an adult to cut down into the rubber around the shape with a craft knife, and then cut the extra part of the rubber away to leave the shape you want.

2 Stamp the rubber on an ink pad and print. Using a rubber to make a stamp gives a smooth finish, like a shop-bought rubber stamp.

PONGE

1 Draw a shape on the sponge with a felt pen. Ask an adult cut round the shape with a aft knife, then cut the extra onge away.

2 Dab the sponge on a plate of paint or fabric paint. Sponge stamps give a varied texture to your motif. Wash the sponge after use.

OTATO

1 Cut a potato in half and draw a shape on one half of the potato th a felt pen. Ask an adult to cut ound the shape with a knife.

2 Stamp the potato on an ink pad and print. If you are printing onto fabric, remember to use a fabric ink pad.

Creating a Picture

You can create a picture in several different ways: you can print lots of different motifs to build up a scene, you can repeat stamps to give a pattern, or you can give the same stamp different colours.

1 Use a selection of different stamps and colours to create a picture or story. This picture is all about sea life. You could even write your own story to go alongside the picture you have created.

2 A repeat pattern can either be very compact like these bones, or very spacious. You can also experiment by using more than one image.

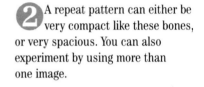

3 If you are worried about printing in a straight line, simply draw a straight line with a ruler and a pencil. This will act as a good guideline and, when your stamping has dried, you can rub out the pencil.

4 You will be amazed at how many different effects you can make from one stamp. For a really colourful effect, you can print the same motif in different inks on different papers, then cut them out carefully and arrange them on a card.

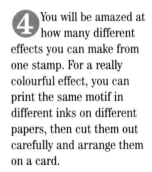

5 Print the motif on paper using a pigment ink, and when it is dry, carefully pipe glitter over some of the motif. Allow this to dry thoroughly as well.

6 If you use pigment ink on its own, use colours that you really like. Choose the colour of the paper carefully, and experiment with different ink colours to create your favourite combinations.

7 A rainbow ink pad gives your stamp several different colours at once. Make sure they will all show up on the paper you choose.

8 With printing felt pens you can colour different parts of the stamp. The stamp was coloured red and green before printing, but the black pips were filled in afterwards.

Paw Print Paper

Create your own designer wrapping paper and matching ribbon to make the presents you wrap up look extra special.

YOU WILL NEED

Paper
Pigment ink pads
Paw print stamp
Ribbon
Sticky tape
Scissors
Scottie dog
  roller stamp

1 Take a large piece of coloured paper and lay it on a smooth at surface. Cover the paper with amped paw prints. You could do ese in rows or at random.

2 Lay the ribbon out on a flat surface. Stick one end down with a piece of strong sticky tape. Smooth the ribbon out, then tape down the other end.

3 Roll the roller stamp on the ink pad then carefully roll it along the ribbon. To cover a long piece of ribbon, you will need to re-ink the stamp. Try and match up the design as carefully as possible each time.

4 When the ink has dried on the paper and ribbon, you are ready to wrap up your present. Tie the ribbon around the parcel and finish with a bow.

Fishy Folders

Give an ordinary file or folder a new look with the following ideas. If your folder is old and tatty, cover it in a fresh piece of paper before you begin. The pocket on the front of the folder is very useful for storing your pens and pencils in.

YOU WILL NEED
Coloured card and paper
Scissors
Glue
File or folder
Fringing
Fish stamps
Pigment ink pads
Shell stamp

1 Cut a piece of coloured card into a rectangle and paint a line of glue along two long sides and a short side. Glue the pocket onto the front of the file and press down gently to make sure it sticks and holds in place.

2 Cut a piece of fringing to fit along the open edge of the pocket and glue it on. You can make your own fringing by clipping into a strip of paper.

3 Cut out lots of paper fish shapes and print the fish stamps onto them. When the ink is dry, glue the shapes onto the file.

You could also glue some cut-out paper fish onto a paper folder, then print shells around them.

Pompom Pencil Pot

Transform a plastic bottle into a container for anything from pencils to wooden spoons. If you have lots of plastic bottles, you could make a set and cover them with different coloured papers.

YOU WILL NEED

Plastic bottle
Tape measure
Craft knife
Scissors
Coloured paper
Dalmatian dog stamp
Pigment ink pad
Double-sided sticky tape
Pompom braid
Glue

1 Draw a straight line around a plastic bottle (at the same height all the way round). Ask an adult to cut it for you. Keep the bottom half.

2 Measure the height of the bottle and then measure roun it with a tape measure. Cut a piece of paper to the same height, but ad 5 mm to the length to give an overla Lay the paper on a smooth flat surface and print the stamp all over it. Leave the ink to dry.

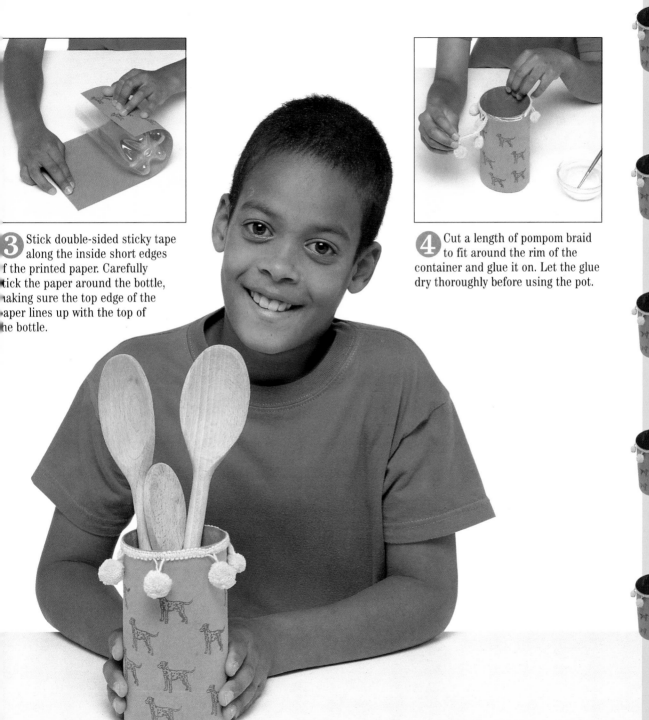

3 Stick double-sided sticky tape along the inside short edges of the printed paper. Carefully stick the paper around the bottle, making sure the top edge of the paper lines up with the top of the bottle.

4 Cut a length of pompom braid to fit around the rim of the container and glue it on. Let the glue dry thoroughly before using the pot.

Starry Pillowcase

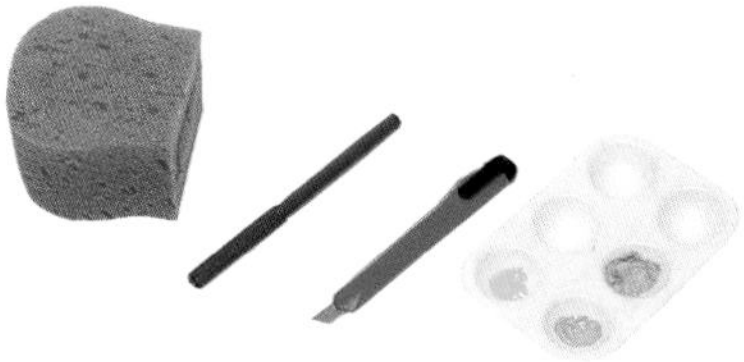

Turn your skills to a bit of textile printing and re-design your pillowcase. If you are feeling adventurous, why not decorate your duvet cover to match your pillowcase?

YOU WILL NEED

Sponge
Felt pen
Craft knife
Old paper
Plain pillowcase
Fabric paint
Old plate
Iron

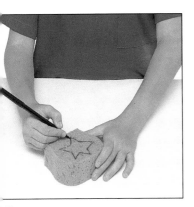

1 Draw a star on a smooth sponge with a felt pen.

2 Ask an adult to cut around the star using a craft knife. Keep the left-over pieces of sponge as they might come in useful for making another sponge stamp.

3 Place an old piece of card or paper inside the pillowcase and lay it on a flat, smooth surface. Pour some fabric paint onto an old plate and dab the sponge in it. Press the sponge gently on the pillowcase to make a print. Re-apply the paint to the sponge for each print.

4 When you have covered the first side of the pillowcase with your prints, leave the paint to dry thoroughly. Turn the pillowcase over and do the same to the other side. When the pillowcase is finished and the paint is completely dry, ask an adult to iron over the design to set the paint.

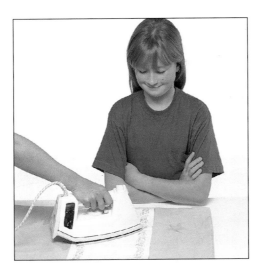

Covered Boxes

This project shows you how to jazz up card boxes. Recycle boxes by covering them with decorated paper. They're brilliant for storing all your odds and ends in.

YOU WILL NEED

Coloured paper
Scissors
Pig stamp
Chicken stamp
Pigment ink pads
Boxes to recycle
Glue

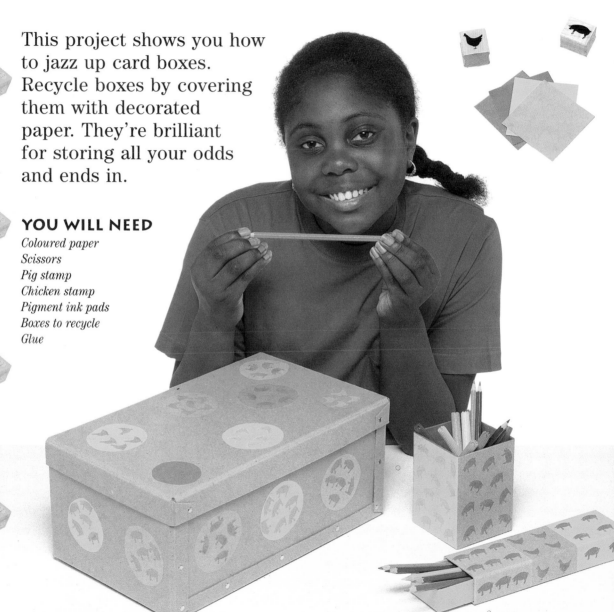

1 Cut out circles of paper in lots of bright colours.

2 Stamp each circle with the pig or chicken stamp, using brightly coloured inks that contrast with the paper. Leave the ink to dry.

3 Arrange the circles where you want them before glueing them onto your box.

4 You can also completely cover lots of different boxes with coloured paper and then print onto the paper.

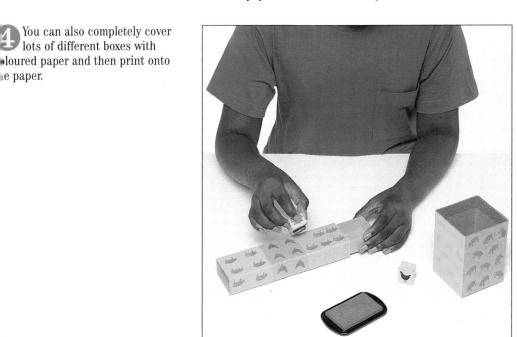

Lovely Letters

Your friends will enjoy reading a letter from you all the more if it's on stylish designer paper.

YOU WILL NEED
Envelope
Coloured paper
Ruler and pencil
Glue
Scissors
Rocket stamp
Pigment ink pads
Globe stamp
Cat's-eye ink pads
White stickers

1 If you're not sure how to make an envelope, simply take one that hasn't been used and open the seams out. Place it on a coloured piece of paper and draw around it. Fold it in the right places and glue the sides to hold it together, but leave the top flap open. Decorate the front of the envelope with stamp prints, too, if you want to.

2 Cut out a piece of writing paper from coloured paper, making it the same width as the envelope and twice as long. Lay it on a smooth flat surface. Decorate around the edge of the paper with stamps to match the envelopes. Leave the ink to dry.

3 Use the cat's-eye ink pads to colour the globe stamp and then print onto a plain white sticker For each print you will need to re-apply the ink.

4 When the ink has dried, cut around the globe and use it to seal the envelope after you have written your letter.

25

Flower **C**ards & **T**ags

Friends and family are always delighted to receive a home-made card or gift tag on their present. Why not print the same design you print on the cards onto a piece of coloured paper to make matching wrapping paper?

YOU WILL NEED

Sunflower stamp
Pigment ink pads
Coloured paper
Scissors
Glue
Ruler
Hole punch
Ribbon

1 Stamp the sunflower onto coloured pieces of paper. If you are using a mixture of different coloured inks, remember to wash the stamp between each colour.

2 Cut around the sunflower and glue it onto a colourful luggage label. You can make your own label out of card. Punch a hole at the top of the gift tag with a hole punch.

3 To make a greetings card, fold piece of coloured paper in half and glue a sunflower onto the front. See how creative you can be by making as many different cards and gift tags as possible.

26

4 To thread the ribbon through the gift tag hole, fold the ribbon in half, push the folded end through the hole, then pull the other end through the loop. Tie or stick it onto your present.

Rocket & Star Pot

If you are unable to find a terracotta flowerpot at home, you can buy one from most garden centres and hardware stores. This project shows you how you can turn the flowerpot into a designer container for your odds and ends or for a plant.

YOU WILL NEED

Terracotta flowerpot
Acrylic or emulsion paint
Paintbrush
Rocket stamp
Pigment ink pads
Home-made rubber stamp
Varnish

1 Cover the surface you are working on with newspaper or an old cloth to avoid making a mess. Paint the outside of the pot (except the rim) a bright colour. Leave the paint to dry thoroughly.

2 Paint the inside of the pot and the rim a contrasting colour to the outside. Leave the paint to dry again.

3 With a very steady hand, print the rocket around the rim of the pot, being careful not to slip. You might want to ask an adult or a friend to hold the pot for you.

4 Cut a home-made rubber stamp into the shape of a star, and use it to print on the outside of the pot. Leave the ink to dry thoroughly and then varnish the pot. It is important to do this if you are going to put a plant in the pot.

Fringed **P**arty **C**ups

Drinking out of these fun cups will cause great excitement at your tea party!

YOU WILL NEED
Plastic or paper cups
Coloured paper
Ruler
Scissors
Cow roller stamp
Pigment ink pads
Double-sided sticky tape

1 Measure and cut out a piece of colourful paper for the fringe ... g enough to fit round the plastic ...ps and 5 cm deep.

2 Roll the stamp on the ink pad then roll it along one edge of the strip of paper you have just cut out. Leave the ink to dry.

3 Cut a fringe along the other edge of the paper by making evenly spaced cuts that are the same length. Do not cut into the stamps.

4 Stick a strip of double-sided sticky tape on the back of the paper behind the row of cows. Peel the back of the double-sided tape off and stick the paper around the rim of the cup. You might need the help of an adult or a friend to hold the cup steady while you do this.

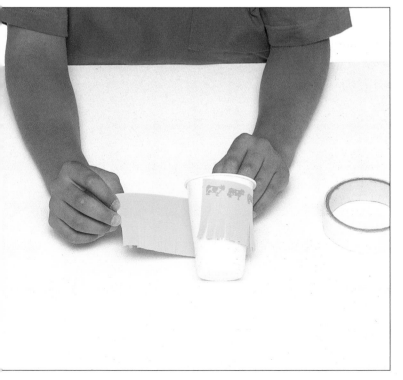

Fruity **T**-shirt **& S**horts

This outfit is perfect for the summer when the sun is shining and it's nice and warm outdoors. Your friends will be so impressed by your new outfit they will be wondering where you bought it!

YOU WILL NEED

T-shirt
Old paper
Fabric inks
Fabric ink pads
Strawberry stamp
Watermelon stamp
Shorts
Iron

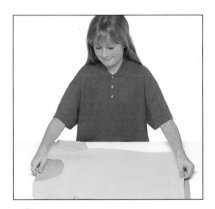

1 Lay the T-shirt flat on a covered work surface with a piece of paper inside it. This will prevent the print going through to the other side of the T-shirt and making a mess.

2 Using fabric ink, print strawberries all over the front of the T-shirt. Print watermelons in the spaces between the strawberries. Leave the inks to dry thoroughly before trying on the T-shirt.

3 Place your shorts flat on the work surface and print strawberries round the legs. Remember to re-ink the stamp so that the strawberries look the same.

4 When the ink has dried on both the T-shirt and shorts, ask an adult to iron them for you (with a paper towel under the iron) to set the ink.

Spotty Cushion Cover

Add some colour to a plain cushion cover by painting lots of spots onto it and printing on top of them with a potato print.

1 Ask an adult to cut a potato in half, and with a felt pen draw a spot on one half of the potato. Then ask an adult to cut around the spot with a knife.

2 Cover the surface you are working on with newspaper and lay the cushion cover flat. Place a piece of newspaper inside the cushion cover to separate the two sides. Paint large spots on the fabric. Leave the paint to dry.

3 Dab the potato on the ink pad and print onto the painted spots. Do this to all the spots.

4 When the ink is completely dry, ask an adult to iron over the spots to set the ink and paint.

Sea Frieze

Decorate a wall with this magical frieze full of exciting sea life. Ask an adult before you start the project just in case they want to help you.

YOU WILL NEED

Coloured paper squares
Large piece of card
Glue
Pigment ink pads
Shell stamps
Seaweed stamps
Fish stamps
Octopus stamp

1 Stick the coloured squares of paper next to each other along a wall or on a length of card. Make sure the ends join up neatly.

2 Starting with the shell stamps, print along the bottom edge of the squares. It is a good idea to stand back from your work every so often so you can see how the story is progressing and to check that you are printing in the right place.

3 Print the seaweed stamp along the squares above the shells. Print some on the joins between the coloured squares.

1 Print the fish and other creatures in-between the ~~s~~aweed and the shells. Leave the ~~in~~ks to dry thoroughly before ~~to~~uching the frieze.

37

Gift Bag

This bag is a fun way of wrapping up a gift for someone you love! Change the size of the bag to match the present, but make sure your present isn't too heavy otherwise it might break the bag.

YOU WILL NEED

Coloured paper
Ruler
Scissors
Glue
Hole punch
Ribbon
Strawberry stamp
Printing felt pens

38

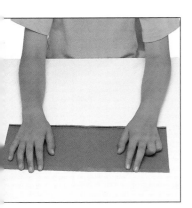

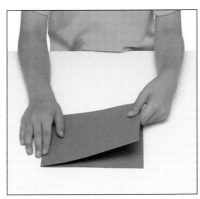

1 Measure and cut out a piece of paper 30 by 13.5 cm. Fold the paper in half and open it out again. Fold over each long side by 5 mm.

2 Paint a line of glue along the folded edges. Fold the paper in half, pressing the sides firmly so that they stick together.

3 Punch two holes through the top of the bag about 5 cm apart from each other. Cut two lengths of ribbon 20 cm long and thread each one through a set of the punched holes, tying a knot at the ends to keep them secure.

4 To make rubber stamps print in different colours, use the printing felt pens to colour the leaves green and the strawberry red. Stamp the strawberry onto a piece of paper. You will need to re-colour the strawberry stamp for each print. Cut out the strawberries and glue them onto the bag.

Party Napkins

Decorate your party table with your own designer paper napkins. Why not stamp each napkin in a different style for each friend?

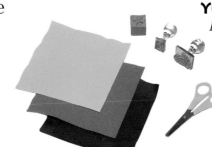

1 Decorate some of the napkins by clipping a fringe around the edge. Be careful if you are using sharp scissors.

2 On the other napkins cut zigzags or spikes around the edges. Make sure they are even.

3 Lay each napkin on a smooth flat, covered surface and stan a row round the edges. Make sure t stamps are evenly spaced and that they are level with each other.

4 Fill in the centre with different stamped prints to your own design. Leave each napkin to dry thoroughly before you lay them on your party table.

41

Flower **P**ower **L**eggings

Decorate a plain pair of leggings with lots of different flowers. You can use colours that blend in or contrasting colours that match a T-shirt.

YOU WILL NEED

Plain coloured leggings
Old paper
Set of flower stamps
Fabric ink
Fabric stamp pads
Iron

42

  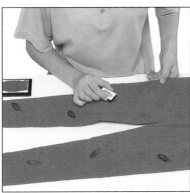

1 Cover the surface you are working on with paper. Lay the leggings flat on the surface. Cut a piece of paper to fit up inside each leg and at the top.

2 Using fabric ink, print flowers on the leggings. Remember to print all over the fabric, as when you have the leggings on they will stretch and the stamps will spread out a bit.

3 Print some leaves in a contrasting colour between the flowers. Leave the ink to dry.

4 Ask an adult to iron over the flowers to set the ink. After that the leggings are ready to wear!

Bug Socks

Shock your friends with these creepy-crawly socks. Remember to use cotton socks so that you can iron them to set the ink.

YOU WILL NEED
Plain coloured socks
Bug stamps
Fabric ink
Fabric ink pad
Iron

44

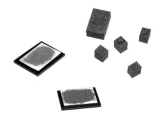

① Cover the surface you are working on with paper or an old cloth and lay the sock flat. Print the spider all over the socks.

② Print the smaller bugs around the spiders. When the ink has dried, turn the socks over and do the same to the other side.

③ If you print on a different coloured pair of socks, you can then wear the odd socks together!

④ When the ink has dried thoroughly, ask an adult to iron each sock under a paper towel to set the ink, otherwise the bugs might crawl off!

Blossoming Lamp Shade

Make bedtime reading fun by decorating your bedside lamp. Be very gentle when you are printing onto a lamp shade, as the surface isn't very firm and you don't want to slip and smudge your design.

YOU WILL NEED

Pen
Felt
Scissors
Glue
Lamp shade
Flower stamp
Fabric inks
Fabric ink pads
Paintbrush and paints

1 Draw flower shapes on pieces of coloured felt and cut them out. Cut out contrasting spots for the centres and glue them on the flowers.

2 Glue the felt flowers onto the lamp shade, pressing them on with one hand and holding the back of the lamp shade with the other.

3 Carefully apply the flower stamp to the lamp shade in-between the felt flowers using a mixture of coloured inks.

4 If your lamp shade has a base, you could paint it a bright colour to match the flowers or paint stripes on it. Leave it to dry before attaching the lamp shade to it. Ask an adult to help you fit a bulb before you plug it in and light up!

47

Watermelon Bin

If you think this bin looks too good to put your rubbish in, you could store your odds and ends in it.

YOU WILL NEED
Coloured paper
Watermelon stamp
Pigment ink pads
Scissors
Plain waste paper bin
Paintbrush and paints
Glue
Home-made rubber stamp

1 Stamp watermelon shapes onto different coloured paper using an assortment of coloured inks. Remember to wipe the melon clean between each new colour.

2 When the ink has dried, cut around the printed melons.

3 Paint the bin in one colour, and paint the corners in a contrasting colour. When the paint has dried, glue the melon shapes onto the bin and leave to dry.

4 Using a home-made stamp made from a rubber, stamp the inside of the bin. If your bin is metal this will not work, so print the shape onto pieces of paper first and then stick them on.

49

Stamped Scarf

You can wear this fun scarf around your neck or in your hair. You could make your own scarf to print on by cutting out a square piece of plain fabric, folding over the edges and sewing them down.

YOU WILL NEED

Large white scarf or
piece of fabric
Different motif stamps
Fabric inks
Fabric ink pads
Iron

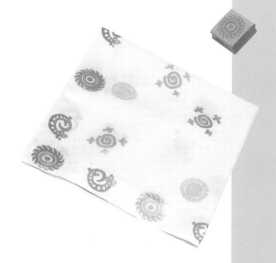

1 Cover the surface you are working on with an old cloth or a piece of newspaper. Spread the scarf flat on the surface and stamp the same image in the four corners of the scarf.

2 Using different coloured inks, stamp different motifs around the edge of the scarf.

3 Scatter more motifs in different colours in the middle of the scarf, and leave the inks to dry.

4 When the inks have dried, place an old piece of cloth on an ironing board and place the scarf on top of it with the right side facing down. Ask an adult to iron it all over and this will set the inks.

5 When you choose the ink colours for your stamps, try to match them to some clothes you already have so that you can team up your new scarf with your wardrobe.

Butterfly Pencil Case

Make your very own pencil case using pieces of felt. If you dislike sewing you could always use fabric glue to hold the sides together and sticky pieces of Velcro to fasten the pencil case.

YOU WILL NEED

Square of felt
Needle
Thread
Fabric glue
Poppers
Scraps of coloured felt
Butterfly stamp
Fabric ink
Fabric ink pad

1 Fold the square of felt as shown in the photograph and sew along each side using a simple running stitch, or carefully glue a strip down the sides with fabric glue.

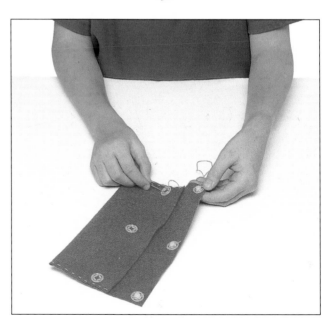

2 Sew on three poppers underneath the top flap of the pencil case and directly opposite on the facing piece of felt (*right*).

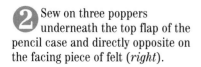

3 Cut out three squares of felt, each in a different colour, and ⬛amp a butterfly print onto each ⬛e. Leave the ink to dry. Cut out the ⬛tterfly shapes.

4 Glue each butterfly along the outside flap of the pencil case to hide the stitching for the poppers.

53

Mini-Beast Drawers

If you have an old cupboard or small piece of furniture, why not give it a lick of paint and stamp some fun images onto it? Remember that painting can be messy, so cover the surface you are working on with lots of newspaper or an old cloth.

YOU WILL NEED

Set of mini drawers
Emulsion paints
Paintbrush
Set of bug stamps
Bumblebee stam
Pigment ink pa

1 If you are painting a small chest of drawers, remove the drawers from the frame. Paint the frame a bright colour and leave the paint to dry thoroughly. You might need to put on two coats of paint. Ask an adult for advice.

2 Paint each drawer separately and leave the paint to dry.

3 When the drawers have dried, put them back in the frame. In each drawer print a different selection of bugs.

4 Print the bumblebee stamp around the frame of the chest of drawers. Leave the inks to dry before you put all your odds and ends back in the drawers.

Doodle Print Pumps

Give a pair of pumps a new look by printing fun patterns all over them. You could also replace the plain shoelaces with bright pieces of ribbon to add an extra splash of colour.

YOU WILL NEED

Plain coloured pumps
Newspaper
Set of doodle stamps
Fabric inks
Fabric stamp pads
Fabric glitter glue
Ribbon

1 Fill each pump with scrunched-up newspaper. Press it in quite firmly. This will make the pumps easier to print on.

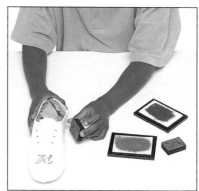

2 Print the doodle stamps on the pumps, pressing very gently. It might help if you slip one hand in behind the spot where you want to stamp. Leave the ink to dry.

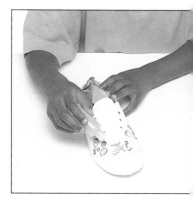

3 Decorate the pumps with fabric glitter glue in funny shapes or small spots. Leave the glue to set.

4 Thread a brightly coloured piece of ribbon through the lace holes of each pump. They are now ready to try on and dance around in.

57

Cactus Tea Towel

This tea towel will definitely spice up the kitchen, and it makes a great present.

YOU WILL NEED

Plain tea towel
Cactus stamps
Fabric inks
Fabric stamp pads
Chilli stamp
Iron

58

1 Lay the tea towel flat on a well-covered surface and print one sort of cactus around the edges with 10 cm gap between each print.

2 Using a different cactus stamp, print in-between the shapes you have just printed around the edges of the tea towel.

3 Scatter-print chilli shapes in the middle of the tea towel. Leave the inks to dry thoroughly.

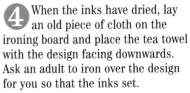

4 When the inks have dried, lay an old piece of cloth on the ironing board and place the tea towel with the design facing downwards. Ask an adult to iron over the design for you so that the inks set.

Swirly Bag

This project shows you how to make a rope print block. As well as using this bag for laundry, you could use it for your sports gear or as a holiday bag.

YOU WILL NEED

Card
Scissors
Cotton cord
Glue
Pillowcase
Needle
Thread
Old paper
Paintbrush
Fabric paint
Ribbon
Safety pin

1 Cut a piece of card in a square. Cut a length of cord and glue it in a circle onto the card, holding it down until it feels secure. Cut a small strip of card and fold it in half. Glue one half onto the print block to form a handle.

2 With the pillowcase right side out, fold over the opening edge by 5 cm and sew it down all around with a line of running stitches.

3 Place a piece of paper inside the pillowcase to separate the two sides and lay it on a flat surface. Paint the cord with fabric paint and press it down firmly on the fabric. You will need to re-apply the paint onto the cord for each print. When you have covered the fabric with the prints, leave the paint to dry and then print on the other side.

4 Cut a length of ribbon about three times the width of the pillowcase. Pin the safety pin to one end of it. Snip a hole in the tube you have just sewn around the opening of the pillowcase and thread the ribbon through it. Tie the two ends in a knot and pull the ribbon to close the bag.

61

Flowery Frame

You can put a photograph of your favourite animal or friend or a piece of your artwork in this fun frame and hang it on your bedroom wall.

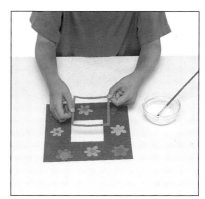

1 Using a ruler, measure a piece of card 20 cm by 20 cm and cut it out. Measure a square 8 cm by 8 cm in the centre of the frame and ask an adult to cut it out with a craft knife.

2 Draw flowers on different coloured papers, and cut them out. Cut circles for the centres of the flowers and glue them on.

3 Glue the flowers onto the frame. Ask an adult to cut a thin frame of coloured paper to go around the hole in the centre of the frame. Glue it on carefully.

4 Stamp the butterfly shapes around the frame between the flowers and leave the ink to dry.

5 Cut out a square piece of card 10 cm by 10 cm and stick it onto the back of the frame with sticky tape, leaving one edge open to put the photograph or picture in. Cut a short piece of ribbon and fold it in half. Stick it onto the top edge of the frame with a piece of sticky tape and hang the finished picture on the wall.

63

ACKNOWLEDGEMENTS

The Publishers would like to thank the following manufacturers for providing the rubber stamps and other materials for this book:

First Class Stamps:
Fish (pages 16–17 and 36–37), seaweed (pages 36–37), flowers (pages 42–43 and 46–47), doodles (pages 56–57).

Inca Stamp:
Paw print (pages 14–15), shell (pages 16–17), pig and chicken (pages 22–23), globe (pages 24–25), sunflower (pages 26–27), octopus, shell, group of shells (pages 36–37), and bumblebee (pages 54–55).

Make Your Mark:
Dalmatian (pages 18–19), rocket (pages 24–25 and 28–29), dragon and pig (pages 40–41), butterfly (pages 62–63).

Rubber Stampede:
Scottie dog roller stamp (pages 14–15), cow roller stamp (pages 30–31), Watermelon and strawberry (pages 32–33, 38–39 and 48–49),

bug (pages 44–45 and 54–55), motifs (pages 50–51), butterfly (pages 52–53), chillies and cacti (pages 58–59).

The Publishers would also like to thank the following children (and their parents!) for modelling for the book:

Kristina Chase, Leoni Hughes-Brown, Lana Green, Lee Johnson, Reece Johnson, Janel Kiamil, Mai-Anh Peterson, Alexandra Richards, Leigh Richards.